I-Spy

Alphabet Soup

A Phonics Reader

By Sasha Quinton

The Book Shop, Ltd.
New York, New York

© 2009 The Book Shop, Ltd
Photographs © Juniperimages Corporation

Let's play **I-Spy!**
What can you **find?**
Try to **spy** a fun **surprise.**

Can you spy:
five chicks and two
shiny telescopes?
How many
eyeglasses can
you spy?

Look up **high.**
Look down low.
It **might** be **right**
before your **eyes!**

I spy little boxes and bags.
Some are tall and some
are **wide.**

Can you **spy:**
a **striped** bag
and a **lime**
green bow?

Each one is just the **right size**,
For a cat to **hide inside.**

I spy some playful pups!
They each wear a **disguise.**

Can you find: a
dinosaur, white
wings, and two
pairs of **eyeglasses**?

Find a **pirate** and his **bride.**
Look for three pups wearing **ties.**

I **spy** some **tiny mice.**
I see one on a ball of **twine.**

Can you find:
a **die**, melon **rind**,
and three **slices**
of cheese?

Find three **mice** on a **tightrope,**
And **five** more in a **line.**

I spy a **spider** in a heart.
What's that **inside** a **light?**

Do you **spy:** a **white** bowl, a **lime-green** can, and a **driving** gerbil?

I spy a pup with a pizza **pie.**
Find a frog on a **bright** blue **kite.**

I spy baskets full of fun.
Yikes! I see two with snakes inside!

Hiss!

Find: a butterfly,
shy beagle,
white yarn, and
two mice.

One has **five** bunnies,
and one has **five** pups.
I spy a basket **lying** on its **side.**

I spy fluffy ducks and chicks.
Count the eggs with birds **inside.**

Can you find: a frying pan, tiny worm, and a chick inside a can?

One small chick is **dyed bright** pink.
Find five more standing **side-by-side.**

What fun! Let's play **I-Spy** again.
See what else you can **spy**.
Look again to find a new **surprise.**
It's not hard if you **try!**

Keep an **eye** out for:
- a black and **white** cow
- a **striped** elf hat
- a stained glass **light**
- a pile of **dimes**

- a **slice** of bread
- a mouse **inside** an apple
- a seagull in **eye** goggles

- a **bright** red slipper
- two **white** kittens in baskets
- a black and **white** spotted pup